Sainsbury's
·RECIPE·LIBRARY·

MEDITERRANEAN COOKING

Carole Handslip

CONTENTS

Published exclusively for J Sainsbury plc
Stamford House Stamford Street
London SE1 9LL
by Martin Books, a division of Woodhead-Faulkner Ltd
Fitzwilliam House 32 Trumpington Street
Cambridge CB2 1QY

INTRODUCTION

Mention Mediterranean cooking and most people will turn to nostalgic thoughts of lazy, sunny days spent enjoying delicious seafood. Fish and, of course, olives do play a large part in Mediterranean cooking, but for me the magic is conjured up by markets blazing with the colours of fruit and vegetables. Huge juicy red tomatoes made memorable with the taste of basil; vivid red, yellow and green peppers; refreshing cucumbers; crisp radicchio and frisé . . . all tossed in the greenest oil of the first olive pressing—to make wonderful salads.

Fish is enormously varied and, although increasing scarcity is making it more expensive, it is still immensely popular. Meat dishes are of rather less importance although there are plenty of interesting lamb dishes to be tried. Vegetables, on the other hand, are varied, full-flavoured and inexpensive. Herbs are an essential ingredient in many recipes. Nothing is wasted. All these things contribute to the robust peasant character of the true Mediterranean kitchen.

Although each country has its own specialities—paella and refreshing gazpacho from Spain, *soupe de poisson* from France and the familiar Greek feta salad (*Horiatiki*)—many typically Mediterranean dishes can be found in different guises all along the coast from Spain to Greece. Further along the coastline are new experiences—couscous, spicy kofta, falafel and a thousand different *mezze*. Most of these eastern Mediterranean and North African dishes trace their origins to Syria.

For me Mediterranean cooking evokes so many pleasurable memories of crisp *calamares* in bustling beach cafés, of markets and bazaars, sounds, smells and laughing faces. Wonderful flavours which I shall never forget.

NOTES

Ingredients are given in both metric and imperial measures. Use either set of quantities but not a mixture of both in any one recipe.

All spoon measurements are level:
1 tablespoon = one 15 ml spoon
1 teaspoon = one 5 ml spoon.

Ovens should be preheated to the temperature specified.

Freshly ground black pepper is intended where pepper is listed.

Fresh herbs are used unless otherwise stated. If unobtainable dried herbs can be substituted in cooked dishes but halve the quantities.

Eggs are standard size 3 unless otherwise stated.

FIRST COURSES

This chapter contains a variety of appetizers and soups. In Turkey and the Middle East it is common for a selection of *mezze* or appetizers to be served together as a first course: choose from Taramasalata, Baba Ghanoush, Turkish Bean and Marrow Salad, Borek and Hummus. Many of the vegetable dishes and salads (pages 52–71) make ideal starters so look to these pages too, when planning a first course.

TARAMASALATA

GREECE

75 g (3 oz) bread
juice of 1 lemon
75 g (3 oz) smoked cods'
roe, skinned
2 cloves garlic, crushed

3 tablespoons olive oil
lemon wedges to garnish
olives and pitta bread to
serve

Serves 6
Preparation time:
15 minutes
Freezing:
Recommended

1. Place the bread in a small bowl, pour over 3 tablespoons water, press down well and leave to soak for 10 minutes.
2. Turn into a food processor or blender, add the remaining ingredients and work together until very smooth.
3. Garnish with lemon and serve with olives and warm pitta bread.

PAN AMB OLI

SPAIN

I first had this at a little restaurant in an old mill in the middle of Menorca. It was made with Serrano ham, however Parma ham makes an equally delicious substitute.

2 cloves garlic, crushed
2 tablespoons extra virgin
olive oil
4 thick slices crusty bread

1 ripe Beefsteak tomato
4 slices Parma ham
salt and pepper to taste
parsley sprigs to garnish

Serves 4
Preparation time:
10 minutes
Freezing:
Not recommended

1. Soak the garlic in the oil and set aside.
2. Toast the bread lightly on both sides.
3. Cut the tomato in half and press the cut surface firmly into each piece of toast so that it turns pink and gathers a few seeds. Discard the tomato shell.
4. Sprinkle with the garlic flavoured oil, and salt and pepper, then lay a slice of Parma ham on top. Garnish with parsley to serve.

BABA GHANOUSH

SYRIA

This aubergine dip is popular all over the Middle East. Grill the aubergines over charcoal if possible—it gives them a delicious smoky flavour that blends well with the tahini. Serve with fingers of pitta bread.

*3 aubergines, halved
   lengthways
2 cloves garlic, crushed
4 tablespoons tahini
juice of 1 lemon
½ teaspoon ground
   cumin*

*salt and pepper to taste
TO GARNISH:
1 tablespoon chopped
   parsley
few black olives*

Serves 6–8
Preparation time:
30 minutes
Freezing:
Recommended

1. Prick the aubergines all over with a fork and place cut side down on a greased baking sheet.
2. Grill them slowly for about 15 minutes, until the skins are black and start to blister and the flesh feels soft.
3. Scoop out all the flesh, place in a blender or food processor with the remaining ingredients and work together until smooth.
4. Divide between individual plates, sprinkle with the parsley and garnish with olives.

TURKISH BEAN AND MARROW SALAD

TURKEY

A delicious dish cooked for me by a Cypriot friend. It should be made with fresh black-eye peas cooked in the pod, but these are difficult to find in England so French or Dwarf beans may be substituted. The dish can be eaten hot as an accompaniment, but I prefer it cold as a first course.

*750 g (1½ lb) French or
   Dwarf beans, cut into
   2.5 cm (1 inch) lengths
750 g (1½ lb) marrow,
   peeled, seeded and cut
   into 1 cm (½ inch)
   cubes*

*5 tablespoons olive oil
juice of ½ lemon
1–2 cloves garlic, crushed
salt and pepper to taste*

Serves 6–8
Preparation time:
10 minutes
Cooking time:
15 minutes
Freezing:
Recommended

1. Cook the beans in boiling salted water for 5 minutes. Add the marrow and cook for 10 minutes. Drain thoroughly and place in a bowl.
2. Add the remaining ingredients and stir well. Leave to cool. Serve with pitta bread.

BOREK

Borek are little pastries made with very fine sheets of pastry and filled with white cheese, spinach or minced meat. They are rolled into several different shapes and deep-fried, or brushed with butter and baked in the oven. In Turkey the pastry is called *yufka* and is sold in large discs. It's not available here so use fillo pastry instead.

275 g (9 oz) fillo pastry (9 sheets)	*FOR THE FILLING:*
	200 g (7 oz) Feta cheese
4 tablespoons olive oil for brushing	*2 tablespoons each chopped parsley and dill*
	3 tablespoons milk

Makes about 45
Preparation time:
45 minutes
Cooking time:
10–15 minutes
Freezing:
Recommended;
reheat to crisp
before serving

1. First make the filling. Mash the cheese with the herbs, adding the milk to bind.
2. Cut each sheet of pastry crossways into 5 strips, measuring 7.5 × 25 cm (3 × 10 inches) and stack on top of each other to prevent them from drying.
3. To make cigarette shapes, brush the pastry strips one at a time with oil and place a little filling at one end. Roll up a few times, then fold in the sides to seal in the filling. Continue to roll, without folding in the sides.
4. To make triangles, brush the pastry strips with oil and place a little filling at one end. Fold over one corner to make a triangle. Continue folding the pastry strip from side to side keeping the shape of a triangle until the pastry is used up.
5. Place the pastries on baking sheets and brush with oil. Bake in a preheated oven, 190°C/375°F/Gas Mark 5, for 10–15 minutes, until golden. Serve warm.

VARIATION

Replace the Feta filling with 1 tablespoon olive oil, 1 small onion, chopped finely, 150 g (5 oz) minced beef, ½ teaspoon cumin, 2 tablespoons chopped parsley and salt and pepper to taste. Heat the oil in a pan, add the onion and fry until softened. Add the minced beef and cook, stirring, for about 10 minutes, adding the cumin for the last minute. Stir in the parsley, and salt and pepper and leave to cool slightly. Continue as above.

HUMMUS

MIDDLE EAST

This purée of chick peas has an earthy flavour much relished throughout the Middle East. A classic dish, originally from Syria, it is also popular in the Lebanon, Israel and Jordan. The purée keeps very well in a covered container in the refrigerator.

*250 g (8 oz) dried chick
    peas, soaked overnight
4 tablespoons tahini
1 teaspoon ground cumin
2–3 cloves garlic, crushed
juice of 1–2 lemons
salt and pepper to taste*

*TO FINISH:
1 tablespoon olive oil,
    blended with 1 teaspoon
    paprika
1 tablespoon chopped
    parsley*

Serves 8
Preparation time:
15 minutes
Cooking time:
About 1 hour
10 minutes
Freezing:
Recommended

1. Drain the chick peas, place in a large pan and cover with cold water. Bring to the boil and boil rapidly for 10 minutes, then cover and cook for 1 hour, until soft. Drain, reserving 300 ml (½ pint) of the cooking water.
2. Place the chick peas, tahini, cumin, 2 cloves garlic, the juice of 1 lemon, and a little salt and pepper in a food processor or blender. Add enough of the reserved liquid to blend to a soft, creamy paste.
3. Check the seasoning, adding more garlic and lemon juice to taste.
4. Turn into a shallow bowl and smooth the surface with the back of a spoon, making swirls as you do so. Dribble over the blended oil, sprinkle with the parsley, and serve with warm pitta bread.

ANCHOÏADE

FRANCE

A rustic preparation of anchovies and oil, ideal to serve with drinks. Accompany it with black olives, if you wish. Soaking the anchovies in milk helps remove the saltiness.

*2 × 50 g (1¾ oz) cans
    anchovies, drained and
    soaked in milk
2 cloves garlic, crushed*

*1–2 tablespoons olive oil
½ teaspoon wine vinegar
8 thick slices crusty bread,
    toasted*

Serves 8
Preparation time:
15 minutes
Freezing:
Recommended

1. Chop the anchovies finely, then pound in a mortar with the garlic. Gradually mix in enough olive oil to thin the mixture slightly, then add the vinegar.
2. Spread the toast with the anchoïade, pressing in well.

SOUPE DE POISSON

All along the Mediterranean inexpensive fish, mainly small and bony, are sold specifically for soup. Even without such variety, we can achieve a good result using fish such as gurnard, conger eel, shad, mullet and a few shellfish.

This soup is traditionally served with *rouille*—a piquant spread which is smeared onto toasted French bread, sprinkled with Parmesan, then dropped into the soup.

3 tablespoons olive oil
1 onion, chopped
1 kg (2 lb) mixed fish (see above), cut into chunks
2 cloves garlic, crushed
125 g (4 oz) shrimps
4 tomatoes, skinned and chopped
2 teaspoons tomato purée
few fennel sprigs
1 bouquet garni
few saffron strands
1.2 litres (2 pints) water
50 g (2 oz) vermicelli, broken into short lengths (optional)

salt and pepper to taste
FOR THE ROUILLE:
½ small red pepper, cored and seeded
2 cloves garlic, chopped
2 red chillies, deseeded and chopped
50 g (2 oz) fresh breadcrumbs
2 tablespoons fish stock or water
120 ml (4 fl oz) olive oil
TO SERVE:
Parmesan or Gruyère cheese, grated
toasted French bread

Serves 6
Preparation time:
50 minutes
Cooking time:
About 25 minutes
Freezing:
Recommended for soup only

1. Heat the oil in a heavy-based pan, add the onion and cook until just turning golden. Add the fish and garlic, and cook for 5 minutes, stirring frequently, until the fish begins to take colour.
2. Add the shrimps, tomatoes, tomato purée, fennel, bouquet garni, saffron, water, and salt and pepper. Bring to the boil, cover and simmer for 20 minutes.
3. Meanwhile, make the rouille. Grill the red pepper, cut side down, until the skin blackens; wash off the black skin. Put the garlic, chillies, red pepper, breadcrumbs, stock or water and salt to taste in a food processor and work until smooth. Gradually add the oil through the feeder tube; 1 or 2 teaspoons at a time. Set aside.
4. Remove any large pieces of bone, then strain the soup through a coarse sieve, pressing the fish and bones thoroughly so as much flavour and flesh as possible is extracted.
5. Return to the pan, bring to the boil, add the vermicelli if using, and cook for about 5 minutes.
6. Serve with the rouille, cheese and French bread.

AVGOLEMONO

This egg and lemon soup is probably the best known of all Greek soups. It can be made with beef or fish stock, if you prefer.

GREECE

1.2 litres (2 pints) chicken stock	*2 eggs*
50 g (2 oz) long-grain rice	*juice of 1 lemon*
	salt and pepper to taste

1. Bring the stock to the boil in a large saucepan. Add the rice, cover and cook for about 15 minutes, until tender. Season with salt and pepper.
2. Beat the eggs and lemon juice together, then whisk in a little of the boiling stock. Gradually add to the saucepan, stirring constantly over a very gentle heat; do not allow to boil or the eggs will curdle. Serve immediately.

Serves 4–6
Preparation time:
5 minutes
Cooking time:
20 minutes
Freezing:
Not recommended

HARIRA

This nourishing chick pea and vegetable soup is the national soup of Morocco. It is eaten during Ramadan— the Moslem month-long period of fasting. When the signal is given at dusk, their daily fast is broken with this soup.

125 g (4 oz) dried chick peas, soaked overnight and drained
2 tablespoons oil
250 g (8 oz) lamb, cubed
1 onion, chopped
125 g (4 oz) dried red lentils
397 g (14 oz) can chopped tomatoes

1 teaspoon ground ginger
few saffron strands
50 g (2 oz) long-grain rice
1 red pepper, cored, seeded and chopped
2 tablespoons chopped parsley
salt and pepper to taste
lemon wedges to serve

Serves 6
Preparation time:
15 minutes, plus soaking time
Cooking time:
1½ hours
Freezing:
Recommended

1. Cook the chick peas in a large pan of rapidly boiling water for 10 minutes. Drain.
2. Heat the oil in a pan, add the lamb and fry until sealed. Add the onion and fry gently until softened. Add the chick peas and 1.5 litres (2½ pints) water. Cover and cook gently for 1 hour.
3. Add the remaining ingredients, cover and cook for about 30 minutes. Serve with lemon wedges.

SOUPE AU PISTOU

A delicious vegetable soup, served with a paste of basil, garlic and Parmesan, which is stirred into it as it is served. The pistou can be made in a food processor, if you prefer.

125 g (4 oz) dried haricot beans, soaked overnight
3 tablespoons olive oil
2 leeks, white part only, sliced thinly
2 carrots, chopped
1 turnip, chopped
125 g (4 oz) French beans, cut into 2.5 cm (1 inch) lengths
175 g (6 oz) courgettes, chopped
125 g (4 oz) broad beans

4 tomatoes, skinned and chopped
1 tablespoon tomato purée
50 g (2 oz) macaroni
salt and pepper to taste
FOR THE PISTOU:
25 g (1 oz) basil leaves
2 cloves garlic
½ teaspoon coarse salt
50 g (2 oz) Parmesan cheese, grated
6 tablespoons olive oil

1. Drain the haricot beans, place in a large pan and cover with cold water. Bring to the boil and boil rapidly for 10 minutes, then cover and simmer gently for 30 minutes. Drain, reserving the water; make up to 1.5 litres (2½ pints) with water.

2. Heat the oil in a large pan, add the leeks and fry until softened. Add the carrots and turnip and cook for 2 minutes.

3. Add the haricot beans and reserved liquid, cover and cook for 45 minutes. Add the remaining ingredients and cook for 30 minutes.

4. Meanwhile, make the pistou. Place the basil, garlic and salt in a mortar and pound with a pestle until it is reduced to a coarse purée. Add half of the cheese and pound together, then mix in a little oil to moisten. Continue adding the cheese and oil until well mixed.

5. Pour the soup into a warmed tureen. Pass the mortar of pistou to each guest to stir a little into their own soup. Alternatively, put the pistou in the bottom of the tureen and pour over the hot soup.

Serves 8
Preparation time:
25 minutes, plus
soaking time
Cooking time:
1 hour 55 minutes
Freezing:
Recommended

AJO BLANCO

SPAIN

This soup is a delicious blend of almonds, bread and garlic, with muscat grapes. Traditionally it is made by pounding the almonds, bread and garlic in a mortar, but now, thank goodness, a blender or food processor will cut out the hard work and speed up the process! The amount of garlic you add depends on your taste and the strength of the garlic.

150 ml (¼ pint) milk
125 g (4 oz) white bread, crusts removed
125 g (4 oz) blanched almonds
3 cloves garlic (see above)
3 tablespoons white wine vinegar

3 tablespoons virgin olive oil
450 ml (¾ pint) water
125 g (4 oz) muscat grapes, peeled, halved and seeded
salt and pepper to taste

Serves 4–6
Preparation time:
15 minutes
Freezing:
Not recommended

1. Pour the milk over the bread and leave to soak for a few minutes. Place in a food processor or blender with the almonds, garlic, vinegar, oil, water, and salt and pepper and work together for 40–50 seconds, until smooth.
2. Place some ice cubes in a soup tureen, pour over the soup and sprinkle with the grapes to serve.

GAZPACHO

This refreshing soup comes from Andalusia. Our tomatoes lack the flavour of sun-ripened Spanish tomatoes, so I often add tomato juice to the soup to compensate.

500 g (1 lb) ripe tomatoes, skinned and chopped
1 small onion, chopped
2 cloves garlic
2 slices white bread, crusts removed, broken into pieces
½ cucumber, peeled and chopped roughly
300 ml (½ pint) tomato juice

3 tablespoons olive oil
2 tablespoons wine vinegar
salt and pepper to taste
TO GARNISH:
1 each small green and red pepper, cored, seeded and diced
1 small onion, chopped
1 hard-boiled egg, chopped
20 croûtons

1. Place the tomatoes, onion, garlic, bread, cucumber, tomato juice, oil, vinegar, and salt and pepper in a blender or food processor and work together until smooth.
2. Stir in 300 ml (½ pint) water, pour into a soup tureen and chill until required.
3. Place the garnishes in separate small dishes.
4. Add ice cubes to the tureen just before serving. Pass the garnishes separately.

Serves 4
Preparation time:
20 minutes
Freezing:
Not recommended

FISH DISHES

LOUP DE MER AU FENOUIL

FRANCE

If possible, this should be cooked over a charcoal fire; place some extra dried fennel on the grid first, which will impart a delicious flavour to the sea bass.

1 kg (2 lb) sea bass
few sprigs of fresh or dried
*   fennel*
6 tablespoons olive oil

salt and pepper to taste
lemon wedges to serve
*   (optional)*

Serves 4
Preparation time:
10 minutes
Cooking time:
20–30 minutes
Freezing:
Not recommended

1. Scale and gut the fish, then make 3 deep diagonal cuts on each side.
2. Season the cavity well, then insert the fennel. Brush the fish well with oil.
3. Cook under a preheated medium grill for 10–15 minutes on each side, basting occasionally with oil.
4. Serve with lemon wedges if you wish.

LANGOSTINA AL AJILLO

SPAIN

King prawns are the largest of the prawn family—they can grow as long as 23 cm (9 inches). This recipe can be made using smaller prawns, but if you use ready-cooked ones they will only need a few minutes in the hot oil to heat them through.

125 ml (4 fl oz) olive oil
8 cloves garlic, chopped
½ dried red chilli, seeds
*   removed*

16 raw King prawns
salt and pepper to taste
lemon slices to serve

Serves 4
Preparation time:
5 minutes
Cooking time:
5 minutes
Freezing:
Not recommended

1. Place the oil, garlic, chilli, and salt and pepper in a shallow flameproof casserole or shallow pan with a lid, and heat until the garlic begins to brown.
2. Arrange the prawns in the casserole or pan and spoon over the flavoured oil. Cover and cook for about 5 minutes, until the prawns have turned pink.
3. Serve with lemon slices and plenty of crusty bread, so that you can mop up all the juices.

SARDINES WITH LEMON AND PARSLEY

GREECE

You will find sardines, or other similar fish, served all along the Mediterranean coast in small fish restaurants. Often they are grilled over charcoal, which gives them a particularly good flavour. Ideal accompaniments are fresh bread and a salad.

1 kg (2 lb) fresh sardines
6 tablespoons olive oil
3 tablespoons lemon juice

2 tablespoons chopped
*   parsley*
salt and pepper to taste
lemon wedges to serve

Serves 4
Preparation time:
15 minutes
Cooking time:
4–6 minutes
Freezing:
Not recommended

1. Scale the sardines thoroughly. Using scissors, cut off the fins, snip off a thin sliver of the belly and remove the intestines. Wash thoroughly and pat dry.
2. Mix the oil, lemon juice, parsley, and salt and pepper together and brush over the fish. Cook under a preheated hot grill for 2–3 minutes, brushing with the oil mixture when they begin to brown. Turn the fish, brush again and grill for a further 2–3 minutes.
3. Transfer to a warmed serving dish, pour over the remaining oil mixture and serve with lemon wedges.

ZARZUELA DE MARISCOS

SPAIN

Zarzuela means musical comedy and *Zarzuela de Mariscos* is a speciality of Catalonia—a really spectacular way to serve a variety of shellfish. Clams are used in the local dish, but it is not possible to find here the tiny ones called coquinas, which have such a special flavour, so I have used extra mussels instead. Don't forget the finger bowls!

2 small cooked lobsters,
*   each weighing 500 g*
*   (1 lb)*
8 raw King prawns
3 tablespoons olive oil
1 onion, chopped
2 tablespoons brandy
2 cloves garlic, chopped
4 ripe Beefsteak tomatoes,
*   skinned and chopped*
300 ml (½ pint) white
*   wine*

50 g (2 oz) blanched
*   almonds, ground*
few saffron strands, soaked
*   in 2 tablespoons boiling*
*   water*
1 bay leaf
24 mussels, cleaned (see
*   Moules à la Provençale,*
*   page 26)*
2 tablespoons chopped
*   parsley*
salt and pepper to taste
lemon wedges to serve

1. Cut the lobsters in half: insert a sharp knife into the little cross on the shell, about 3.5 cm (1½ inches) above the point where the tail joins the body. Cut in half lengthways.

2. Remove the sac from the head and the intestinal vein, but leave the brown liver and black coral if there is any. Twist off the claws, discarding the smaller ones.

3. Shell the prawns, leaving the tailpiece attached.

4. Heat the oil in a large shallow casserole, add the onion and fry until softened, then pour in the brandy. Add the garlic, tomatoes, wine, ground almonds, saffron, bay leaf, and salt and pepper. Cover the casserole and simmer gently for 5 minutes.

5. Add the lobsters, prawns, mussels and parsley, cover and cook for 5 minutes, until the lobsters are heated through, the prawns turn pink and the mussels open; discard any mussels that do not open and crack open the lobster claws.

6. Transfer to a warmed shallow dish, discarding the bay leaf. Serve with lemon wedges.

Serves 4
Preparation time: 20 minutes
Cooking time: About 10 minutes
Freezing: Not recommended

ROUGETS À LA NIÇOISE

FRANCE

A typical way of serving red mullet in Nice. The scales of red mullet are very tough and must be scraped off thoroughly, using the back of a knife, working from the tail to the head. Red mullet are often left uncleaned as the flavour is said to be better when they are cooked this way. I prefer to clean the fish, but retain the liver for the flavour it imparts.

2 tablespoons olive oil	*4 red mullet, scaled and*
1 onion, chopped	*cleaned, but retaining*
2 cloves garlic, crushed	*the liver (see above)*
4 tomatoes, skinned and	*50 g (2 oz) black olives,*
chopped	*pitted*
2 teaspoons tomato purée	*2 tablespoons chopped*
125 ml (4 fl oz) white wine	*parsley*
1 bouquet garni	*salt and pepper to taste*

Serves 4
Preparation time:
15 minutes
Cooking time:
20 minutes
Freezing:
Not recommended

1. Heat the oil in a flameproof casserole, add the onion and cook until softened. Add the garlic, tomatoes, tomato purée, wine, bouquet garni, and salt and pepper, cover and cook gently for 10 minutes.
2. Arrange the mullet in the sauce and sprinkle with the olives and parsley. Cover and cook gently for 10 minutes.
3. Transfer the fish to a warmed serving dish and spoon over the sauce to serve.

FRITTO MISTO MARE

ITALY

This fried mixed fish dish is served all over Italy in various forms: it may consist of 3 or 4 different fish, or as many as a dozen. The ingredients may be coated in egg and bread-crumbs, a batter or simply tossed in seasoned flour. They are then deep-fried until crisp and golden and served immediately. You could include sole, eel, octopus or scampi in this recipe if you wish.

350 g (12 oz) small squid	*seasoned flour*
4 small red mullet	*oil for deep-frying*
4 fresh sardines	*2 lemons, cut into wedges,*
8 raw prawns	*to serve*

1. Clean and cut the squid into 2.5 cm (1 inch) wide rings; leave the tufts of tentacles whole if small, otherwise cut them in half.

2. Scale and clean the red mullet, but leave the liver inside the fish to give a better flavour.

3. Scale the sardines and cut off the fins. Snip off a thin sliver of the belly and remove the intestines. Wash thoroughly and pat dry.

4. Dip the fish into seasoned flour and deep-fry immediately in hot oil: fry the red mullet two at a time for about 4 minutes, depending on size, drain on kitchen paper and keep warm; fry the sardines for about 3 minutes, drain and keep warm; fry the prawns and the squid for about 2 minutes.

5. Arrange all the fish on warmed plates and serve immediately, with the lemon wedges.

Serves 4
Preparation time:
20 minutes
Cooking time:
About 15 minutes
Freezing:
Not recommended

MOULES À LA PROVENÇALE

Toulon is renowned for its mussels and this recipe offers them in a delicious saffron and wine sauce.

2 kg (4½ lb) mussels
125 ml (4 fl oz) white wine
2 tablespoons olive oil
1 onion, chopped finely
1 clove garlic, crushed
1 tablespoon plain flour
2 teaspoons tomato purée

3 tomatoes, skinned and
* chopped finely*
1 bouquet garni
few saffron strands
2 tablespoons chopped
* parsley*
salt and pepper to taste

Serves 4
Preparation time:
30 minutes
Cooking time:
About 15 minutes
Freezing:
Not recommended

1. To clean the mussels scrub them thoroughly, removing the beards and discarding any mussels that stay open when tapped.
2. Place the wine in a large pan and bring to the boil. Add the mussels, cover tightly and cook briskly for 2–3 minutes, until they open; discard any that do not. Strain off the liquid and reserve. Discard the empty half shell from each mussel.
3. Heat the oil in a pan, add the onion and fry until just beginning to turn golden. Add the garlic and cook for 1 minute. Stir in the flour and tomato purée, then blend in 300 ml (½ pint) of the reserved liquor.
4. Add the tomatoes, bouquet garni, saffron, and salt and pepper. Bring to the boil and cook quickly for 10 minutes, uncovered so that it reduces slightly.
5. Add the mussels and parsley, mix with the sauce and heat through gently—do not overcook or the mussels will become tough. Discard the bouquet garni. Serve hot, with crusty French bread.

INSALATA DI MARE

A mixture of shellfish, served in a light lemony dressing —very popular as a starter or main course in Italy.

250 g (8 oz) baby squid
5 tablespoons olive oil
4 scallops
500 g (1 lb) mussels,
* cleaned (see Moules à la*
* Provençale, above)*

250 g (8 oz) peeled prawns
* (thawed if frozen)*
3 tablespoons lemon juice
2 tablespoons chopped
* parsley*
salt and pepper to taste

1. Cut the squid into rings and leave the clusters of tentacles whole.

2. Heat 1 tablespoon of the oil in a small pan, add the squid tentacles and rings and cook, stirring, for 1–2 minutes. Add 6 tablespoons water, cover and simmer gently for 8–10 minutes. Add the scallops and cook for 4 minutes. Remove the squid and scallops with a slotted spoon and leave to cool.

3. Add the mussels to the pan, cover tightly and cook briskly for 2–3 minutes, until they open; discard any that do not. Remove from their shells and place in a bowl.

4. Separate the white part of the scallops from the coral and slice into discs. Add both to the mussels, with the squid and prawns.

5. Mix the remaining oil, lemon juice, parsley, and salt and pepper together, pour over the shellfish and leave to marinate for 30 minutes before serving.

Serves 3 as a main course, 6 as a starter
Preparation time: 25 minutes, plus marinating
Cooking time: 15–20 minutes
Freezing: Not recommended

KALAMARI KRASATA

GREECE

Squid dishes similar to this are found throughout the Mediterranean.

1 kg (2 lb) squid
3 tablespoons olive oil
1 onion, chopped
150 ml (¼ pint) red or
  white wine

4 tomatoes, skinned and
  chopped
2 tablespoons chopped
  parsley
salt and pepper to taste

Serves 4–8
Preparation time:
20 minutes
Cooking time:
45–50 minutes
Freezing:
Recommended

1. Cut the body of the squid into 1.5 cm (¾ inch) slices and the tentacles into 2.5 cm (1 inch) lengths.
2. Heat the oil in a pan, add the onion and fry until softened. Add the squid and cook for a few minutes, until it becomes firm and pink. Add the remaining ingredients and cook for 45–50 minutes, until the squid is tender.
3. Serve cold with crusty bread as a starter for 8, or hot with rice as a main course for 4.

TAGLIATELLE CON COZZE

ITALY

1.75 kg (4 lb) mussels,
  cleaned (see Moules à la
  Provençale, page 26)
3 tablespoons olive oil
1 onion, chopped finely
2 cloves garlic, crushed
1 tablespoon tomato purée

397 g (14 oz) can chopped
  tomatoes
350 g (12 oz) tagliatelle
2 tablespoons chopped
  parsley
salt and pepper to taste

Serves 4
Preparation time:
30 minutes
Cooking time:
About 10 minutes
Freezing:
Not recommended

1. Place the mussels in a large pan, add 6 tablespoons boiling water, cover tightly and cook briskly for 4 minutes, until they open; discard any that do not. Remove from their shells, leaving a few intact for garnish. Strain the liquor and set aside.
2. Heat 2 tablespoons of the oil in a pan, add the onion and fry until softened. Add the garlic, tomato purée, tomatoes, 125 ml (4 fl oz) of the reserved liquor, and salt and pepper. Bring to the boil and cook, uncovered, for about 10 minutes, until reduced slightly.
3. Meanwhile, cook the tagliatelle according to packet instructions. Drain and toss in the remaining oil.
4. Add the parsley and mussels to the sauce, and heat through, gently. Arrange the pasta on a warmed serving dish, pour over the sauce and garnish with the reserved mussels. Serve immediately.

PAELLA MARINERA

SPAIN

Paella is renowned throughout the world, but the ingredients differ enormously in various parts of Spain. The best known version includes chicken with seafood and is called *Paella a la Valenciana*. The traditional Valencian paella contains only snails and green beans. Others may include rabbit, quail, meatballs or sausages. One of the best I have eaten was in a small restaurant perched above the sea in Javea, which included only fish and shellfish —this is my version of it.

1 cooked lobster, weighing 625 g (1¼ lb)
5 tablespoons olive oil
350 g (12 oz) monkfish, cut into 2.5 cm (1 inch) cubes
250 g (8 oz) squid, cut into rings
1 onion, chopped
2 cloves garlic, chopped
4 tomatoes, skinned and chopped roughly
500 g (1 lb) Valencian rice or Italian risotto rice
1 litre (1¾ pints) fish stock or water

125 g (4 oz) frozen peas
few saffron strands, soaked in 2 tablespoons boiling water
1 red pepper, grilled, skinned and cut into strips
16 mussels, cleaned (see Moules à la Provençale, page 26)
175 g (6 oz) prawns in shell
2 tablespoons chopped parsley
salt and pepper to taste
lemon wedges to serve

Serves 6
Preparation time:
45 minutes
Cooking time:
About 35 minutes
Freezing:
Not recommended

1. Prepare the lobster as for *Zarzuela de Mariscos* (page 22), then cut the tail into 5 cm (2 inch) pieces.
2. Heat 2 tablespoons of the oil in a large paella pan or shallow flameproof casserole, add the monkfish and squid rings and tentacles to the pan and fry for 2 minutes, turning constantly. Remove with the juices, and set aside.
3. Heat the remaining oil in the pan, add the onion and garlic and fry until softened, stirring frequently.
4. Add the tomatoes and cook for 2 minutes, then sprinkle in the rice, stirring until it is well coated.
5. Pour in the stock or water, add the peas, saffron, and salt and pepper and mix well. Stir in the monkfish, squid and red pepper and push the mussels into the rice.
6. Cook in a preheated oven, 180°C/350°F/Gas Mark 4, for about 25 minutes, until the liquid is absorbed but the rice not quite done.
7. Ten minutes before the end of cooking, discard any unopened mussels, arrange the lobster and prawns on top

of the rice and return to the oven. Remove from the oven, cover the dish with foil and leave to stand for 10 minutes. Crack open the lobster claws. Sprinkle with the parsley and serve with lemon wedges.

TAGINE OF FISH

MOROCCO

A tagine is a shallow, round earthenware dish with a tall cone-shaped lid, in which stews of all sorts are simmered. *Harissa*, a fiery red pepper paste, would be used to flavour this tagine in Morocco—I have substituted cayenne pepper. You can use any type of fish.

3 tablespoons olive oil
2 onions, chopped
2 cloves garlic, chopped
1 red pepper, cored, seeded and sliced
1 teaspoon paprika
1/2 teaspoon cayenne pepper
1 teaspoon turmeric
1 teaspoon cumin powder
397 g (14 oz) can chopped tomatoes
350 g (12 oz) potatoes, cut into chunks

250 g (8 oz) cod, skinned and cut into large chunks
250 g (8 oz) monkfish, cut into large chunks
250 g (8 oz) squid, cut into rings
125 g (4 oz) peeled prawns (thawed if frozen)
4 tablespoons chopped parsley
2 tablespoons lemon juice
salt to taste

Serves 4–6
Preparation time: 20 minutes
Cooking time: 35 minutes
Freezing: Not recommended

1. Heat the oil in a large saucepan, add the onions and fry until softened. Add the garlic, red pepper and spices and cook for 1 minute. Add the tomatoes, potatoes, 900 ml (1½ pints) water, and salt, bring to the boil, then simmer for 15 minutes.
2. Add the cod, monkfish and squid, cover and cook for 15 minutes.
3. Add the prawns, parsley and lemon juice and cook for 5 minutes. Serve immediately with bread.

FISH PLAKI

GREECE

Baking is a method of cooking widely used in Greece for any type of fish—I particularly like cod or haddock treated in this way.

750 g (1½ lb) fish, skinned and cut into serving pieces
juice of 1 lemon
3 tablespoons olive oil
1 large onion, sliced
2 cloves garlic, crushed

250 g (8 oz) tomatoes, skinned and chopped
1 tablespoon tomato purée
125 ml (4 fl oz) white wine
2 tablespoons chopped parsley
salt and pepper to taste

1. Arrange the fish in a shallow ovenproof dish and sprinkle with the lemon juice, and salt and pepper.
2. Heat the oil in a pan, add the onion and fry until softened. Add the garlic, tomatoes, tomato purée and wine, cover and simmer for 15 minutes. Stir in the parsley.
3. Pour the sauce over the fish, cover with foil and cook in a preheated oven, 180°C/350°F/Gas Mark 4, for 35–40 minutes. Serve hot.

Serves 4
Preparation time: 15 minutes
Cooking time: 35–40 minutes
Freezing: Not recommended

MEAT DISHES

TAGINE OF LAMB

MOROCCO

Moroccans have a sweet tooth and many of their tagines contain spices and fruits of all types: dates, prunes, apricots, pears and quinces, as well as honey or sugar. I prefer them without the sugar, so have adapted this one to suit.

125 g (4 oz) dried apricots
125 g (4 oz) pitted prunes
1 aubergine, cut into
*   fingers*
6 tablespoons olive oil
750 g (1½ lb) lean lamb,
*   cut into chunks*
2 onions, sliced
1 each red and green
*   pepper, cored, seeded*
*   and sliced*

½ teaspoon ground
*   ginger*
1 teaspoon ground
*   cinnamon*
600 ml (1 pint) stock or
*   water*
25 g (1 oz) butter
50 g (2 oz) blanched
*   almonds*
salt and pepper to taste

Serves 4–6
Preparation time:
30 minutes, plus
standing time
Cooking time:
1½ hours
Freezing:
Recommended

1. Leave the apricots and prunes to soak in water. Place the aubergine in a colander, sprinkle with salt and leave to stand for 30 minutes. Rinse and dry with kitchen paper.
2. Heat half of the oil in a large flameproof casserole, add the meat and fry to seal. Remove from the pan and set aside.
3. Add the aubergine to the casserole and fry until golden, adding more oil as necessary. Remove from the pan and set aside.
4. Add the remaining oil, onions and peppers and fry, stirring frequently, until they are beginning to brown. Sprinkle in the spices and cook for 1 minute.
5. Add the stock or water, and salt and pepper, bring to the boil, then add the lamb. Cover and simmer very slowly for 1 hour.
6. Drain the apricots and prunes, add to the stew with the aubergine and cook, uncovered, for 30 minutes, until the sauce has reduced.
7. Meanwhile, heat the butter in a small pan, add the almonds and fry until golden. Sprinkle them over the stew and serve with rice.

Illustrated top
right: Moroccan
Spit-roast Lamb
(page 37)

LAMB AND VEGETABLE COUSCOUS

MOROCCO

Couscous is a speciality in many North African countries. The couscous is steamed over a stew, which may include lamb or chicken and various vegetables and spices.

4 tablespoons olive oil
750 g (1½ lb) lamb, cubed
2 onions, sliced
125 g (4 oz) dried chick peas, soaked overnight and drained
2 cloves garlic, crushed
¼ teaspoon saffron strands
2 carrots, quartered
250 g (8 oz) pickling onions, blanched and peeled

2 turnips, quartered
125 g (4 oz) broad beans
500 g (1 lb) couscous
3 courgettes, sliced
4 tomatoes, skinned and quartered
50 g (2 oz) raisins
3 tablespoons chopped parsley
1 teaspoon cayenne pepper
1 teaspoon paprika
salt and pepper to taste

Serves 6
Preparation time:
30 minutes, plus soaking time
Cooking time:
About 2 hours
Freezing:
Not recommended

1. Heat half of the oil in a large saucepan over which you can later fit a strainer or steamer. Add the lamb and fry until sealed, remove and set aside. Add the sliced onions to the pan and fry gently until softened.
2. Pour in 1.2 litres (2 pints) water, add the chick peas, garlic, saffron, and salt and pepper and bring to the boil. Cover and boil rapidly for 10 minutes. Reduce the heat, add the meat, cover and simmer gently for about 1 hour.
3. Add the carrots, pickling onions, turnips and broad beans, mix well and cook for 20 minutes.
4. Meanwhile, place the couscous in a bowl, cover with water and leave to soak for 15 minutes; drain thoroughly.
5. Add the courgettes to the stew. Place the couscous in a strainer or steamer, fit over the saucepan, making sure that the bottom of the strainer does not touch the stew, and steam, uncovered, for 20 minutes.
6. Turn the couscous into a bowl, sprinkle with a little cold water, the remaining oil and salt. Stir well with a fork to break up any lumps and separate the grains. Add the tomatoes, raisins and parsley and mix well. Return to the strainer, fit over the stew and steam for 15 minutes.
7. Take 150 ml (¼ pint) sauce from the stew and stir in the cayenne and paprika.
8. To serve, pile the couscous in a mound on a large warmed serving dish. Place the meat in a depression on top, arrange the vegetables down the sides, and spoon over the liquor. Serve the peppery sauce in a small bowl. Diners help themselves with a large spoon.

MOROCCAN SPIT-ROAST LAMB

Lamb spit-roasted over charcoal *mechoui-style* with its crisp brown crust and moist, tender inside is superb. You could also use an oven spit or simply roast the lamb.

MOROCCO

2–2.5 kg (4½–5 lb) leg of
   lamb
FOR THE MARINADE:
75 g (3 oz) butter, softened
2 teaspoons ground cumin

*1 tablespoon ground
   coriander*
1 teaspoon paprika
1 teaspoon salt
3 cloves garlic, sliced
mint and rosemary sprigs

Serves 6–8
Preparation time:
10 minutes, plus
marinating
Cooking time:
1½–1¾ hours
Freezing:
Not recommended

1. Mix the butter, spices and salt together and rub over the lamb. Make deep incisions at regular intervals in the lamb and insert the garlic and herb sprigs. Cover and leave to marinate for at least 4 hours.
2. Fix the joint onto the spit and roast over a preheated barbecue, or in a preheated oven, 200°C/400°F/Gas Mark 6, for 1½–1¾ hours, basting every 15 minutes or so. If you are barbecuing the lamb you can start carving the outer slices after about 1 hour and leave the rest of the lamb on the spit to complete cooking.
3. Serve with *Fattoush* (page 64) and bread.

Illustrated on
page 35

KIBBEH

SYRIA/LEBANON

So popular are Kibbeh in the Middle East that nimble 'Kibbeh' fingers were a prime requisite for gaining a good husband. Kibbeh originated in Syria and the Lebanon, but they are now found in various forms throughout the Eastern Mediterranean region. They all have certain ingredients in common—bulgar wheat, minced meat, nuts, herbs and spices—but their preparation, shape, size and method of cooking differ from country to country. This recipe was given to me by a Cypriot friend; she omits the meat, which is often used with the bulgar wheat to form the shell, and she also prefers to use diced lamb instead of the minced lamb normally used for the filling.

500 g (1 lb) bulgar wheat
2 tablespoons olive oil
2 onions, chopped finely
350 g (12 oz) lamb fillet,
    cut into small pieces
1 teaspoon allspice

25 g (1 oz) pine nuts
4 tablespoons chopped
    parsley
salt and pepper to taste
oil for deep-frying
lemon wedges to serve

Serves 6–8
Preparation time:
45 minutes, plus soaking time
Cooking time:
About 4 minutes per batch
Freezing:
Recommended

1. Place the bulgar wheat in a bowl, pour over 1.2 litres (2 pints) boiling water and leave to soak for about 40 minutes, until it is cool enough to handle.
2. Meanwhile, make the filling. Heat the oil in a pan, add the onions and fry until softened. Add the lamb and fry, stirring, for about 10 minutes, then add the allspice, pine nuts, parsley, salt and pepper, and cook for a few more minutes. Leave to cool.
3. Add salt and pepper to the soaked bulgar wheat, then knead it for about 5 minutes until it becomes sticky and will form into a ball.
4. Take a small piece and roll in the palms of your dampened hands to make an egg shape. Make a hole in the middle with your forefinger and form the wheat into a hollow pot shape with fairly thin walls.
5. Fill it with the meat mixture, then pinch the open ends together and make into a pointed oval shape. Repeat with the remaining mixture to make about 22.
6. Deep fry a few at a time in hot oil for about 4 minutes, until golden brown.
7. Drain on kitchen paper and serve with lemon wedges.

NOTE: You may find you have a little bulgar mixture or filling left over, depending on how good you are at shaping the bulgar shells.

LAMB KÖFTE

Köfte—meat balls—are one of the most traditional dishes in Turkey, North Africa and many Eastern Mediterranean countries. The shape and flavouring differ from country to country. Sometimes the köfte are moulded around skewers and barbecued over a charcoal fire, or grilled. Sometimes they are simply fried, as in this recipe. The mixture must be kneaded very thoroughly, until it becomes smooth.

TURKEY

75 g (3 oz) bread	*1 onion, grated*
750 g (1½ lb) minced lamb	*1 teaspoon ground cumin*
	salt and pepper to taste
1 egg, beaten	*plain flour for coating*
1 clove garlic, crushed	*oil for shallow-frying*

1. Soak the bread in water for 5 minutes, then squeeze dry and place in a bowl. Add the remaining ingredients, and mix thoroughly.
2. Take a piece of the mixture the size of a golf ball and roll in your dampened hand to form the shape of a finger. Roll in flour, then shallow-fry in batches in hot oil for 5–6 minutes.
3. Serve with Tzatziki (page 66) and a mixed salad.

Serves 6
Preparation time:
30 minutes
Cooking time:
5–6 minutes per batch
Freezing:
Recommended

BURSA KEBAB

TURKEY

This lamb dish is a speciality of the town of Bursa in northern Turkey. The bread used there is a dimpled flat bread called *pide*—pitta is a good substitute. In Turkey the dish is often finished with a good lashing of browned butter, however I prefer to top it with a less rich topping of green pepper and parsley. Elsewhere in Turkey, this dish is known as *yoğurtlu kebab*.

4 tablespoons olive oil
½ onion, chopped finely
500 g (1 lb) boneless lamb, cut into large chunks
250 g (8 oz) tomatoes, skinned and chopped finely
2 pitta bread

240 g (8 oz) carton Greek strained yogurt
salt and pepper to taste
TO GARNISH:
1 green pepper, cored, seeded and sliced
2 tablespoons chopped parsley

Serves 4
Preparation time:
15 minutes, plus marinating
Cooking time:
6–8 minutes
Freezing:
Not recommended

1. Mix the oil, onion, and salt and pepper together, add the lamb and leave to marinate for about 2 hours.
2. Remove the lamb, reserving the oil and onion, and thread onto skewers; grill for 6–8 minutes, turning once.
3. Meanwhile, heat the oil and onion in a pan and cook until softened. Add the tomatoes and cook for a few minutes, stirring occasionally. Season with salt and pepper and keep warm.
4. Toast the pitta bread, cut into small pieces and arrange on 4 warmed plates. Pour over the tomato mixture, then spoon some yogurt on top.
5. Remove the meat from the skewers and arrange on top of the yogurt. Garnish with the green pepper and parsley and serve immediately.

SHISH KEBAB

GREECE/TURKEY

For these kebabs, pieces of green pepper, onion and tomato are interspersed with the lamb, but frequently the lamb is simply grilled on its own.

750 g (1½ lb) boneless lamb, cut into 3.5 cm (1½ inch) cubes
1 green pepper, cored, seeded and cut into squares

4 tomatoes, quartered
4 small onions, each cut into 6 pieces
2 tablespoons olive oil
salt and pepper to taste
lemon wedges to serve

1. Thread the lamb onto 8 skewers alternately with the green pepper, tomatoes and onions.

2. Place on a grill pan, brush with the oil and season with salt and pepper. Cook under a preheated moderate grill for 3–4 minutes on each side.

3. Serve with a lettuce, tomato and onion salad or *Horiatiki* (page 71) and warmed pitta bread or rice.

Serves 4
Preparation time:
20 minutes
Cooking time:
6–8 minutes
Freezing:
Not recommended

PETTI DI POLLO CON FUNGHI

ITALY

3 tablespoons flour
4 skinless chicken breasts,
    halved horizontally
2 tablespoons olive oil
25 g (1 oz) butter
1 onion, chopped
2 cloves garlic, crushed

150 ml (¼ pint) white
    wine
250 g (8 oz) flat
    mushrooms, sliced
1 tablespoon chopped
    parsley
salt and pepper to taste

Serves 4
Preparation time:
10 minutes
Cooking time:
About 20 minutes
Freezing:
Not recommended

1. Season the flour with a little salt and pepper and use to coat the chicken breasts. Set aside.
2. Heat the oil and butter in a frying pan, add the onion and fry until softened.
3. Add the garlic and the chicken breasts and fry for 2 minutes on each side.
4. Add the wine and salt and pepper to taste, cover and cook gently for about 8 minutes.
5. Stir in the mushrooms and parsley and cook for a further 2 to 3 minutes. Serve immediately.

GIGOT D'AIL

FRANCE

Lamb cooked with garlic is a great favourite in Provence. Although the quantity of garlic used is large, the flavour is surprisingly mild and the texture deliciously creamy.

2 kg (4 lb) leg of lamb
4 cloves garlic, quartered
3 tablespoons olive oil
4 bulbs garlic

125 ml (4 fl oz) white wine
125 ml (4 fl oz) stock
salt and pepper to taste

Serves 6
Preparation time:
10 minutes
Cooking time:
1½–1¾ hours
Freezing:
Not recommended

1. Make incisions in the lamb and press the garlic pieces well into the flesh.
2. Place the lamb in a roasting tin, rub with the oil and sprinkle with salt and pepper. Cook in a preheated oven, 200°C/400°F/Gas Mark 6, for 1½–1¾ hours, or according to your liking, basting occasionally.
3. Meanwhile, blanch the whole garlic bulbs in boiling water for 5 minutes, then drain. Add to the roasting tin for the last 20 minutes of cooking.
4. Transfer the lamb and garlic bulbs to a warmed serving dish. Drain off the oil from the roasting tin, then add the wine and stir well to scrape up any sediment. Add the stock, bring to the boil and reduce a little, then pour into a jug. Serve with potatoes.

SCALOPPINE AL MARSALA

ITALY

A well-loved and very quick veal dish, delicious served with braised chicory.

2 tablespoons plain flour
4 thin veal slices, total
*   weight about 500 g*
*   (1 lb)*
3 tablespoons olive oil

125 ml (4 fl oz) Marsala
4 tablespoons stock
salt and pepper to taste
parsley sprigs to serve

Serves 4
Preparation time:
5 minutes
Cooking time:
8 minutes
Freezing:
Not recommended

1. Season the flour with salt and pepper and use to coat the veal, shaking off the excess.
2. Heat the oil in a large frying pan, add the veal and fry quickly for 3 minutes on each side.
3. Pour in the Marsala and allow to cook for 1 minute. Remove the veal and keep warm.
4. Add the stock to the pan, stir well and cook for a few minutes, until it thickens slightly.
5. Pour over the veal and serve immediately, garnished with parsley.

FEGATO DI VITELLO ALLA SALVIA

ITALY

Calves' liver and sage make a delicious combination. Be sure not to overcook the liver or it will be very dry—it should be pink inside.

2 tablespoons plain flour
500 g (1 lb) calves' liver,
*   sliced thinly*
1 tablespoon olive oil
25 g (1 oz) butter
1 clove garlic, chopped

2 teaspoons chopped sage
125 ml (4 fl oz) stock
3 tablespoons dry Marsala
salt and pepper to taste
sage sprigs to garnish

Serves 4
Preparation time:
10 minutes
Cooking time:
About 5 minutes
Freezing:
Not recommended

1. Season the flour with salt and pepper and use to coat the liver.
2. Heat the oil and butter in a large frying pan, add the garlic and liver and fry quickly for 1–2 minutes on each side.
3. Add the sage and stock and cook for 2 minutes. Remove the liver, place on a warmed serving dish and keep warm.
4. Add the Marsala, and salt and pepper to the pan, bring to the boil, stirring, and boil for 1 minute. Pour over the liver and garnish with sage to serve.

DAUBE DE BOEUF PROVENÇALE

FRANCE

A daube is a stew made with either one large piece of meat, or with the meat cut into large squares. It is flavoured with herbs, vegetables and wine, and cooked very slowly. It is very much a peasant dish and the ingredients vary according to what is available.

3 tablespoons olive oil
1 kg (2 lb) braising beef, cut into 5 cm (2 inch) pieces
125 g (4 oz) piece streaky bacon, derinded and sliced
2 carrots, sliced
1 celery stick, sliced
2 cloves garlic, crushed

1 large bouquet garni
4 tomatoes, skinned and sliced
150 ml (¼ pint) red wine
150 ml (¼ pint) beef stock
50 g (2 oz) black olives, pitted
2 tablespoons chopped parsley
salt and pepper to taste

Serves 4–6
Preparation time:
15 minutes
Cooking time:
3½ hours
Freezing:
Recommended

1. Heat the oil in a large flameproof casserole, add the meat and fry briskly to seal. Add the bacon and fry for 2–3 minutes, then add the remaining ingredients, except the olives and parsley. Bring to the boil, then cover and cook in a preheated oven, 150°C/300°F/Gas Mark 2, for 3 hours.
2. Stir in the olives and cook for 30 minutes.
3. To serve, arrange the meat and vegetables on a warmed serving dish. Remove any fat from the sauce, discard the bouquet garni, then pour the sauce over the meat. Sprinkle with the parsley and serve with pasta, rice or haricot beans.

STIFATHO

GREECE

A delicious and warming stew that can be made with beef, pork, veal or rabbit, but always with a large quantity of small pickling onions.

3 tablespoons olive oil
1 kg (2 lb) veal, cut into large cubes
1 onion, chopped
1 clove garlic, crushed
4 tomatoes, skinned and chopped
150 ml (¼ pint) red wine

3 tablespoons red wine vinegar
1 bay leaf
4 cloves
750 g (1½ lb) small pickling onions
2 tablespoons chopped parsley
salt and pepper to taste

1. Heat the oil in a flameproof casserole, add the meat a little at a time and cook until browned. Remove from the pan and set aside.

2. Add the onion and garlic to the pan and cook until softened. Add the tomatoes, wine, vinegar, bay leaf, cloves, 150 ml (¼ pint) water, and salt and pepper. Bring to the boil, then cover and cook in a preheated oven, 160°C/325°F/Gas Mark 3, for 2 hours, until the meat is tender.

3. Meanwhile, cook the onions in boiling water for 3 minutes. Plunge into cold water, then peel off the skins. Add to the stew with the parsley, and cook for 30–40 minutes.

4. If the stew is too liquid, remove the meat and onions and boil the sauce rapidly to reduce. Discard the bay leaf. Turn into a warmed serving dish.

Serves 6
Preparation time: 30 minutes
Cooking time: About 2½ hours
Freezing: Recommended

CONEJO A LA CAZADORA

SPAIN

I first tasted this dish of rabbit cooked in a wine sauce with ham and mushrooms in a small village in the hills behind Altea. The locals use Serrano ham, but as it is not readily available here I have substituted Parma ham.

3 tablespoons olive oil
1 kg (2 lb) rabbit portions
1 onion, chopped
2 cloves garlic, chopped
175 ml (6 fl oz) white wine
4 tomatoes, skinned and chopped

50 g (2 oz) piece Parma ham, diced
1 bouquet garni
125 g (4 oz) mushrooms, sliced
2 tablespoons chopped parsley
salt and pepper to taste

Serves 4
Preparation time:
20 minutes
Cooking time:
1 hour
Freezing:
Recommended

1. Heat the oil in a flameproof casserole, add the rabbit pieces and brown all over. Remove from the pan and set aside.
2. Add the onion and garlic to the pan and cook until softened. Add the wine, tomatoes, ham, bouquet garni and salt and pepper, then return the rabbit to the pan.
3. Cover and cook in a preheated oven, 180°C/350°F/Gas Mark 4, for about 45 minutes.
4. Stir in the mushrooms and parsley and cook for 15 minutes. Discard the bouquet garni and transfer to a warmed serving dish.

CIRCASSIAN CHICKEN

TURKEY

Known as *çerkez tavuğu* in Turkey, this delicious dish of chicken in a walnut sauce can be served as a first course for 6–8, or as a main course with rice for 4.

1 chicken, weighing about 1.5 kg (3 lb)
1 onion, quartered
1 carrot, quartered
1 bouquet garni
50 g (2 oz) bread, crusts removed

175 g (6 oz) shelled walnuts
1 clove garlic, crushed
salt and pepper to taste
TO GARNISH:
2 tablespoons walnut or olive oil
1 teaspoon paprika

1. Place the chicken, onion, carrot and bouquet garni in a large saucepan. Cover with water, bring to the boil, then cover and simmer gently for about 1 hour, until cooked.

2. Remove the chicken from the pan and leave until cool enough to handle. Remove the flesh from the bones, cut into pieces about 5 × 1 cm (2 × ½ inch) and keep warm. Strain the stock and reserve.

3. Place the bread and walnuts in a food processor and work together until the walnuts are ground. Add the garlic, 250 ml (8 fl oz) of the reserved stock, and salt and pepper. Blend until the mixture is smooth and about the consistency of cream. Pour into a saucepan to reheat, adding a little more stock and seasoning if necessary.

4. Arrange the chicken on a warmed serving dish or individual plates and pour over some sauce. Hand any remaining sauce separately.

5. Mix the walnut or olive oil and paprika together and drizzle over the surface to serve.

Serves 4–8
Preparation time: 20 minutes
Cooking time: About 1 hour
Freezing: Not recommended

PIGEONS NIÇOISE

FRANCE

An excellent method of cooking pigeons, which can sometimes be dry and tough. This dish is delicious served with flageolet beans.

2 tablespoons olive oil
2 plump pigeons
125 g (4 oz) piece streaky bacon, chopped
175 g (6 oz) pickling onions, blanched and peeled
1 tablespoon plain flour
2 cloves garlic, crushed

4 tomatoes, skinned and chopped
1 bouquet garni
125 ml (4 fl oz) red wine
125 ml (4 fl oz) stock
10 black olives, pitted
salt and pepper to taste
1 tablespoon chopped parsley to garnish

Serves 4
Preparation time: 20 minutes
Cooking time: About 1½ hours
Freezing: Recommended

1. Heat the oil in a flameproof casserole, add the pigeons and brown on all sides. Remove from the pan and keep warm.
2. Add the bacon and onions to the pan and fry, stirring, until they begin to turn golden. Stir in the flour.
3. Add the remaining ingredients and bring to the boil. Return the pigeons to the casserole, cover and cook in a preheated oven, 160°C/325°F/Gas Mark 3, for about 1½ hours, until tender.
4. Split the pigeons in half, arrange on a warmed serving dish with the onions and keep warm.
5. Discard the bouquet garni and spoon off any excess fat from the sauce, then boil rapidly to reduce slightly. Pour over the pigeons and sprinkle with the parsley to serve.

BRAISED QUAIL WITH OLIVES

SPAIN

Quail and other game birds are very popular in Spain and are everyday items on restaurant menus. Quail is full of flavour, but it is a tiny bird so you will need two per person.

8 quail
4 tablespoons olive oil
1 onion, chopped
2 cloves garlic, chopped
4 tomatoes, skinned and chopped
150 ml (¼ pint) white wine

2 tablespoons brandy
50 g (2 oz) pitted green olives, halved
2 tablespoons chopped parsley
1 bay leaf
1 thyme sprig
thyme sprigs to garnish

1. Truss each quail by tucking the wing tips under the body. Cross the legs and place each in a slit made on either side of the cavity.
2. Heat half of the oil in a large flameproof casserole, add the quail and fry until browned all over. Remove from the pan and keep warm.
3. Add the remaining oil, onion and garlic to the casserole and fry until softened. Add the remaining ingredients and bring to the boil. Return the quail to the pan, cover and simmer gently for about 25 minutes, until tender.
4. Remove the bay leaf and thyme and transfer to a warmed serving dish. Garnish with thyme to serve.

Serves 4
Preparation time:
25 minutes
Cooking time:
About 25 minutes
Freezing:
Recommended

VEGETABLE DISHES

JUDIAS VERDES CON JAMÓN

SPAIN

This dish of green beans with ham makes an excellent accompaniment to almost any meal. It is also very good served as a first course—hot or cold.

500 g (1 lb) green beans
2 tablespoons olive oil
1 onion, sliced
1 clove garlic, crushed

75 g (3 oz) piece Parma ham, cubed
salt and pepper to taste

Serves 4
Preparation time:
10 minutes
Cooking time:
About 13 minutes
Freezing:
Recommended

1. Cook the beans in boiling salted water for about 8 minutes, until almost tender.
2. Meanwhile, heat the oil in a pan, add the onion and fry until softened. Add the garlic and ham and cook for 1 minute.
3. Add the drained beans, cover and cook for 5 minutes, stirring occasionally. Season with salt and pepper and transfer to a warmed serving dish.

FETTUCCINE AL PESTO

ITALY

Make pesto whenever you can gather together enough basil. Store it in a small jar, covered with a thin layer of oil, in the refrigerator for up to 3 weeks.

25 g (1 oz) basil leaves
25 g (1 oz) parsley sprigs, stalks removed
1 clove garlic, crushed
25 g (1 oz) pine nuts

25 g (1 oz) Parmesan cheese, grated
4 tablespoons olive oil
350 g (12 oz) fettuccine
pepper to taste

Serves 4
Preparation time:
20 minutes
Cooking time:
8 minutes using dried pasta, 3 minutes using fresh
Freezing:
Not recommended

1. Place the basil, parsley, garlic and pine nuts in a blender or food processor and work to a purée.
2. Add a spoonful of cheese, then a spoonful of oil and blend to mix. Continue until you have used them both up. Season with pepper, transfer to a bowl and set aside.
3. Meanwhile, cook the fettuccine according to packet instructions. Remove 2 tablespoons of the boiling water and add to the pesto to dilute and warm it slightly.
4. Drain the fettuccine, stir in the sauce and transfer to a warmed serving dish. Serve immediately.

SPANOKOPITTA

GREECE

2 tablespoons olive oil
2 onions, chopped
1 kg (2 lb) spinach, stalks
   removed, chopped
2 eggs
good pinch of grated
   nutmeg

175 g (6 oz) Feta cheese,
   crumbled
50 g (2 oz) butter, melted
350 g (12 oz) fillo pastry
   (12 sheets)
salt and pepper to taste

Serves 6
Preparation time:
25 minutes
Cooking time:
35–40 minutes
Freezing:
Recommended

1. Heat the oil in a pan, add the onions and fry until softened. Add the spinach and cook, stirring, until it has softened and some of the liquid has evaporated. Leave to cool slightly.
2. Beat the eggs with the nutmeg, and salt and pepper. Add the cheese and the spinach mixture, and mix thoroughly.
3. Butter a 28 × 18 cm (11 × 7 inch) baking tin and line with a sheet of fillo pastry, leaving the edges overhanging. Brush with melted butter and lay another sheet on top. Repeat until you have 5 or 6 layers of pastry.
4. Cover the remaining sheets of fillo with a damp cloth, so that they do not dry and become difficult to handle.
5. Cover the fillo in the baking tin with the spinach mixture, smooth evenly to the edges. Cover with the remaining fillo sheets, brushing each with melted butter as before. Trim all the edges level with the top of the tin.
6. Fold the trimmed edges over the top and brush with butter to seal well.
7. Brush the top with the remaining butter and leave for 5 minutes until set, then cut through the top of the pie, marking it into 6 squares.
8. Bake in a preheated oven, 190°C/375°F/Gas Mark 5, for 35–40 minutes, until crisp and golden. Serve hot or cold.

PATATES YIAHNI

GREECE

Potatoes in tomato sauce, perfect with grilled meat.

3 tablespoons olive oil
2 onions, sliced thinly
2 cloves garlic, crushed
500 g (1 lb) ripe tomatoes,
   skinned and chopped
2 tablespoons tomato
   purée
1 bay leaf

1 thyme sprig
2 tablespoons chopped
   parsley
300 ml (½ pint) stock or
   water
1 kg (2 lb) potatoes, sliced
   thickly
salt and pepper to taste

1. Heat the oil in a flameproof casserole, add the onions and fry until softened. Add the garlic, tomatoes, tomato purée, herbs, stock or water, and salt and pepper and cook for 5 minutes. Add the potatoes and stir well until covered in the sauce.

2. Cook in a preheated oven, 180°C/350°F/Gas Mark 4, for about 1½ hours, until the potatoes are tender and the sauce is thick. Serve hot or cold.

Serves 4
Preparation time:
15 minutes
Cooking time:
About 1½ hours
Freezing:
Not recommended

FALAFEL

EGYPT

This chick pea dish is said to have originated in the kitchens of the Pharaohs and is eaten all over the Middle East. I like the patties with this tahini sauce, and often serve them as a first course or with drinks.

250 g (8 oz) dried chick peas, soaked overnight and drained	*1 teaspoon ground cumin*
1 small onion, chopped	*oil for deep-frying*
25 g (1 oz) fresh breadcrumbs	*FOR THE TAHINI SAUCE:*
3 cloves garlic, crushed	*4 tablespoons tahini*
4 tablespoons chopped parsley	*juice of 1 lemon*
1 teaspoon ground coriander	*1 clove garlic, crushed*
	¼ teaspoon ground cumin
	1 tablespoon chopped parsley
	salt and pepper to taste

Serves 4–6
Preparation time:
15 minutes, plus
soaking time
Cooking time:
4 minutes per
batch
Freezing:
Recommended

1. Put the chick peas, onion, breadcrumbs, garlic and 4 tablespoons water in a food processor or blender and work together until smooth. Turn into a bowl and knead in the parsley and spices. Set aside while you make the sauce.
2. Place the tahini in a bowl and gradually blend in the lemon juice until smooth. Add the remaining sauce ingredients with enough water to mix to a smooth cream.
3. Form the chick pea mixture into balls the size of a walnut and flatten slightly. Deep-fry in hot oil in batches for about 4 minutes, until golden brown.
4. Drain well on kitchen paper and serve hot or cold with the sauce.

TORTILLA PAISANA

SPAIN

Spanish omelette, consisting of potato, onion and egg, is a traditional meal throughout Spain. Good though it is, I rather prefer this one, which includes chorizo sausage, peppers and beans.

4 tablespoons olive oil	*125 g (4 oz) chorizo sausage, chopped*
1 onion, sliced thinly	*125 g (4 oz) cooked green beans, cut into 2.5 cm (1 inch) lengths*
1 red pepper, cored, seeded and chopped	
1 clove garlic, crushed	*4 eggs*
1 large potato, boiled and chopped	*salt and pepper to taste*

1. Heat 2 tablespoons of the oil in a pan, add the onion and fry gently until softened. Add the red pepper and garlic and cook, stirring, for 5 minutes. Add the potato, chorizo and green beans and cook for 5 minutes.

2. Beat the eggs with salt and pepper in a bowl, then add the vegetable and sausage mixture and mix thoroughly.

3. Heat the remaining oil in a 25 cm (10 inch) frying pan and pour in the egg mixture. Cook gently for 3–4 minutes, until the eggs are set enough to turn.

4. Invert a plate over the pan, turn the omelette onto the plate, then slide back into the pan, adding more oil if necessary and cook for 1–2 minutes.

5. Slide the omelette onto a warmed serving plate, cut into wedges and serve immediately.

Serves 3
Preparation time:
15 minutes
Cooking time:
4–6 minutes
Freezing:
Not recommended

PATLICAN TAVA

TURKEY

Fried aubergines are used in many Turkish dishes. This one makes a tasty accompaniment and is often served cold.

2 aubergines, sliced	*TO GARNISH:*
8 tablespoons olive oil	*1 tablespoon pine nuts,*
1 onion, sliced into rings	*toasted*
2 cloves garlic, sliced	*1 tablespoon chopped*
salt and pepper to taste	*parsley*

Serves 4
Preparation time:
10 minutes, plus
standing time
Cooking time:
About 10 minutes
Freezing:
Not recommended

1. Place the aubergines in a colander, sprinkle with salt and leave to stand for 30 minutes to remove the bitter juices. Rinse well and pat dry with kitchen paper.
2. Heat the oil in a pan, add the onion and garlic, reserving a little to garnish, and fry until softened. Remove from the pan and keep warm on a warmed serving dish.
3. Add the aubergines to the pan in batches and fry until golden on both sides. Arrange on top of the onion.
4. Top with the reserved onion, pine nuts and parsley.

VARIATION
Simmer the fried aubergines in a tomato sauce: add 2 cloves garlic, 4 large tomatoes, skinned and chopped, and 2 tablespoons parsley to the pan. Cover and simmer for 10 minutes, stirring occasionally.

ZUCCHINI AL MAIS

ITALY

6 courgettes	*pinch of cayenne pepper*
326 g (11½ oz) can	*50 g (2 oz) Parmesan*
sweetcorn, drained	*cheese, grated*
2 eggs, separated	*salt to taste*

Serves 6
Preparation time:
15 minutes
Cooking time:
25–30 minutes
Freezing:
Not recommended

1. Cook the courgettes in boiling salted water for about 6 minutes; drain.
2. Cut in half lengthways and scoop out some of the inside, leaving a 5 mm (¼ inch) thick shell. Chop the flesh and drain off any liquid. Mix with the sweetcorn, egg yolks, cayenne, three quarters of the cheese, and salt.
3. Whisk the egg whites until stiff, then carefully fold into the sweetcorn mixture.
4. Place the courgette shells in an ovenproof dish, spoon in the filling and sprinkle with the remaining cheese. Cook in a preheated oven, 180°C/350°F/Gas Mark 4, for 25–30 minutes, until risen. Serve immediately.

TOMATO AND COURGETTE TIAN

FRANCE

A tian is a country dish which can be made with many different ingredients. It takes its name from the heavy earthenware dish in which it is cooked.

3 tablespoons olive oil
1 onion, chopped
2 cloves garlic, crushed
1 red pepper, cored, seeded and chopped
250 g (8 oz) courgettes, sliced thinly
4 tomatoes, skinned and chopped
50 g (2 oz) cooked rice

3 eggs, beaten
1 teaspoon chopped thyme
2 tablespoons chopped parsley
1 tablespoon grated Parmesan cheese
1 tablespoon fresh breadcrumbs
salt and pepper to taste

Serves 4
Preparation time:
30 minutes
Cooking time:
40–45 minutes
Freezing:
Not recommended

1. Heat the oil in a frying pan, add the onion and fry until softened. Add the garlic, red pepper and courgettes and cook slowly for 10 minutes, stirring occasionally. Add the tomatoes, rice, eggs, herbs, and salt and pepper and stir well to mix.
2. Turn into a greased 1.2 litre (2 pint) earthenware gratin dish and sprinkle with the cheese and breadcrumbs.
3. Cook in a preheated oven, 180°C/350°F/Gas Mark 4, for 40–45 minutes. Serve hot.

DOLMATHAKIA

GREECE

These are little parcels of spicy rice in vine leaves. They make an unusual and interesting first course, and are ideal for barbecues or to take on picnics. The quantities given will make about 40 stuffed vine leaves, so you will probably have sufficient to freeze some for future use.

250 g (8 oz) packet preserved vine leaves
75 g (3 oz) long-grain rice
1 onion, chopped
2 cloves garlic, crushed
2 tomatoes, skinned and chopped
¼ teaspoon each ground cinnamon and allspice

2 tablespoons chopped dill or mint
2 tablespoons pine nuts
2 tablespoons olive oil
juice of 1 lemon
salt and pepper to taste
lemon wedges to serve

1. Drain the vine leaves and rinse well to rid them of excess salt.

2. Boil the rice for 10 minutes only, then drain. Mix with the onion, garlic, tomatoes, spices, herbs, pine nuts, and salt and pepper.

3. Place a spoonful of the rice mixture on a vine leaf. Fold the stem up over the filling, fold both sides towards the middle, then roll into a small parcel, but not too tightly as the rice will swell a little. Squeeze together firmly. Repeat with the remaining leaves and filling.

4. Line the base of a casserole dish with any spare or torn vine leaves, then pack the stuffed vine leaves on top in layers, wedged closely together so that they do not unroll during cooking.

5. Mix the oil with the lemon juice and 300 ml (½ pint) water and pour over the vine leaves. Cover and cook in a preheated oven, 180°C/350°F/Gas Mark 4, for 1–1½ hours, adding a cupful of water occasionally, if necessary, to replace the liquid which has evaporated.

6. Leave the stuffed vine leaves to cool in the casserole. Serve cold, with lemon wedges.

Serves 6–8
Preparation time:
30 minutes
Cooking time:
1–1½ hours
Freezing:
Not recommended

PISSALADIÈRE

FRANCE

This celebrated onion tart from Nice is sold by the slice in the markets and *boulangeries* of Provence. If substituting dried yeast for fresh, you only need half the quantity.

300 g (10 oz) plain flour
½ teaspoon salt
7 g (¼ oz) fresh yeast
175 ml (6 fl oz) warm water
1 tablespoon oil
FOR THE TOPPING:
4 tablespoons olive oil
2 cloves garlic, crushed

1 kg (2 lb) onions, sliced thinly
1 teaspoon chopped thyme
50 g (1¾ oz) can anchovy fillets, drained and halved lengthways
14 black olives
salt and pepper to taste

Serves 4–6
Preparation time: 20 minutes, plus rising time
Cooking time: 25–30 minutes
Freezing: Recommended

1. Sift the flour and salt into a bowl and make a well in the centre. Cream the yeast with a little of the water and leave until frothy. Add to the flour with remaining water and oil.
2. Mix to a soft dough, then turn onto a floured surface and knead for about 5 minutes, until smooth and elastic. Return to the bowl, cover with a damp cloth and leave to rise in a warm place for about an hour, until doubled in size.
3. Meanwhile, make the topping: heat the oil in a pan, add the garlic and onions, cover and cook very slowly, stirring occasionally, for 30–40 minutes, until very soft but not brown. Add thyme, salt and pepper; leave to cool slightly.
4. Turn the dough onto a floured surface and knead for a few minutes, then roll out into a rectangle and press into a greased 33 × 23 cm (13 × 9 inch) Swiss roll tin.
5. Spread the onion mixture over the dough, then top with anchovies and olives. Leave to rise for 10 minutes.
6. Bake in a preheated oven, 220°C/425°F/Gas Mark 7, for 10 minutes, then lower the heat to 190°C/375°F/Gas Mark 5 and bake for 15–20 minutes. Serve hot or cold.

TUMBET

MALLORCA

500 g (1 lb) aubergines, sliced thinly
150 ml (¼ pint) olive oil
3 cloves garlic, chopped
397 g (14 oz) can chopped tomatoes
1 tablespoon tomato purée
2 onions, sliced

1 each green and red pepper, cored, seeded and sliced
500 g (1 lb) potatoes, boiled and sliced
25 g (1 oz) fresh breadcrumbs
salt and pepper to taste

1. Sprinkle the aubergines with salt, place in a colander and leave to drain for 30 minutes. Rinse well and dry with kitchen paper.

2. Meanwhile, heat 1 tablespoon of the oil in a saucepan, add the garlic and fry gently, without browning, then add the tomatoes, tomato purée, and salt and pepper. Cover and simmer for 15 minutes; set aside.

3. Heat 4 tablespoons of the remaining oil in a frying pan, add the onions and peppers and fry gently for 15 minutes, until softened. Remove from the pan and set aside.

4. Heat the remaining oil in the pan, add the aubergine slices in batches and fry until golden. Remove from the pan and drain off any excess oil.

5. Arrange the aubergines in layers in an ovenproof dish, alternately with the potatoes and the pepper and onion mixture, moistening each layer with the tomato sauce. Season the layers well. Pour any remaining sauce on top and sprinkle with the breadcrumbs.

6. Cook in a preheated oven, 200°C/400°F/Gas Mark 6, for 20 minutes, until golden brown and heated through.

Serves 4–6
Preparation time:
1 hour
Cooking time:
20 minutes
Freezing:
Not recommended

SALADS

PEPERONATA

ITALY

One of the most delicious ways to serve peppers of any colour. This dish will keep for several days, so it is worth making double the quantity.

4 tablespoons olive oil
1 onion, sliced
3 red peppers, cored, seeded and sliced
2 cloves garlic, crushed

6 tomatoes, skinned and sliced
2 tablespoons chopped parsley
salt and pepper to taste

Serves 4–6
Preparation time:
15 minutes
Cooking time:
About 20 minutes
Freezing:
Recommended

1. Heat the oil in a heavy-based pan, add the onion, peppers and garlic and fry gently for about 15 minutes, stirring occasionally.
2. Add the tomatoes, parsley, and salt and pepper and cook for 5 minutes. Leave to cool.
3. Transfer to individual dishes to serve.

FATTOUSH

SYRIA

This salad is served in many Arab countries. It is best to add the bread just before serving to maintain its crispness —substitute 4 slices bread for the pitta bread if you prefer.

4 tomatoes, skinned and chopped
1/2 cucumber, cubed
1 green pepper, cored, seeded and chopped
1 Little Gem lettuce, shredded
5 spring onions, chopped

1 tablespoon each chopped parsley, mint and coriander
1 clove garlic, crushed
5 tablespoons olive oil
juice of 1 lemon
salt and pepper to taste
2 pitta bread, toasted and cut into pieces

Serves 4
Preparation time:
15 minutes
Freezing:
Not recommended

1. Place the tomatoes, cucumber, green pepper, lettuce, spring onions and herbs in a salad bowl.
2. Mix the garlic, oil, lemon juice and salt and pepper together until blended, pour over the salad and toss thoroughly.
3. Stir in the bread just before serving.

TZATZIKI

GREECE

This refreshing salad is well known throughout Greece as an accompaniment to barbecued meats, or simply as an appetizer. A similar dish is served in many Eastern Mediterranean countries, but each has a different name. Dried mint is often used instead of fresh.

½ cucumber, peeled
240 g (8 oz) carton Greek
  strained yogurt
1 clove garlic, crushed

2 tablespoons chopped
  mint
salt and pepper to taste

Serves 4
Preparation time:
10 minutes
Freezing:
Not recommended

1. Grate the cucumber and drain thoroughly through a nylon strainer.
2. Mix the cucumber into the yogurt with the garlic and most of the mint, using a fork, then add salt and pepper.
3. Turn into a bowl and sprinkle with the remaining mint.

SALADE MESCLUN

FRANCE

This is a salad from Provence which originally made use of the edible wild herbs and plants that grow so profusely in the hills. Nowadays a selection of many different cultivated salad plants, such as frisé, lambs' lettuce and radicchio, are added. One particular herb I always try to include is rocket, which has a lovely warm peppery flavour—quite easy to grow, but very rarely seen. Batavia, watercress or chicory may be used to replace any of the salad ingredients listed below which you have trouble finding.

½ head frisé (curly endive)
small head radicchio
125 g (4 oz) lambs' lettuce
few dandelion leaves
50 g (2 oz) purslane
few rocket sprigs

FOR THE DRESSING:
4 tablespoons olive oil
1 tablespoon white wine
  vinegar
1 teaspoon Dijon mustard
2 cloves garlic, crushed
salt and pepper to taste

Serves 6
Preparation time:
10 minutes
Freezing:
Not recommended

1. Tear the frisé (curly endive) and radicchio into manageable-sized pieces and place in a salad bowl.
2. Discard the roots from the lambs' lettuce and add to the bowl with the dandelion leaves, purslane and rocket.
3. Place the dressing ingredients in a small screw-top jar and shake thoroughly until blended.
4. Pour over the salad and toss just before serving.

CAPRESE

A very quick salad of tomato and Mozzarella, delicious as a first course for 4 or a light lunch with crusty bread for 6. Make sure the tomatoes are really ripe and find a good quality Mozzarella.

ITALY

500 g (1 lb) Beefsteak tomatoes, sliced
2 Mozzarella cheeses, sliced

3 tablespoons French dressing
2 tablespoons chopped basil

Arrange the tomatoes and Mozzarella in overlapping slices on a round serving dish. Pour over the dressing and sprinkle with the basil to serve.

Serves 4–6
Preparation time: 10 minutes
Freezing: Not recommended

SALADE NIÇOISE

FRANCE

This French salad has become internationally popular probably because it looks good, tastes better, and may be adapted to take advantage of seasonal produce. It makes an excellent first course or, served with lots of crusty bread, a substantial lunch dish.

1 small crisp lettuce
500 g (1 lb) tomatoes, cut into wedges
198 g (7 oz) can tuna, drained and flaked
1 small onion, sliced thinly
2 hard-boiled eggs, quartered

½ cucumber, sliced
50 g (1¾ oz) can anchovy fillets, drained and halved lengthways
50 g (2 oz) black olives, halved and pitted
6 tablespoons French dressing

Serves 4
Preparation time:
15 minutes
Freezing:
Not recommended

1. Arrange the lettuce leaves in 4 individual bowls, then top with the remaining salad ingredients.
2. Add the dressing just before serving.

SALADE TIÈDE

FRANCE

Tiède is French for warm, and a *salade tiède* is a cold salad containing warm meat or fish. Chicken livers are particularly suited to this treatment—delicious rich meat offset by crisp leaves and the special sharpness of raspberry vinegar. Serve as a starter or with lots of warm, crusty bread as a superb summer meal.

175 g (6 oz) young spinach leaves
small head of radicchio
3 tablespoons olive oil

250 g (8 oz) chicken livers
3 tablespoons raspberry wine vinegar
salt and pepper to taste

Serves 4
Preparation time:
About 15 minutes
Freezing:
Not recommended

1. Trim the stalks from the spinach, tear into pieces and place in 4 individual bowls. Tear the radicchio into pieces and divide between the bowls.
2. Heat the oil in a frying pan, add the chicken livers and fry for 3–4 minutes until still pink. Remove from the pan, cut into slices and divide between the salads.
3. Quickly add the vinegar to the pan, stir to blend in any juices and pour over the salads. Season with salt and pepper and serve immediately.

TABBOULEH

This is a very popular dish in all Arab countries. It consists of cracked wheat, known as bulgar wheat, which is already partially cooked, and a variety of fresh herbs.

MIDDLE EAST

175 g (6 oz) bulgar wheat
4 spring onions, chopped
6 tablespoons chopped mint
6 tablespoons chopped parsley

juice of 1 lemon
4 tablespoons olive oil
2 tomatoes, skinned and chopped
salt and pepper to taste

1. Soak the wheat in boiling water for 20 minutes. Drain through muslin and squeeze as dry as possible.
2. Place in a mixing bowl with the remaining ingredients and toss together thoroughly.
3. Turn into a shallow serving dish or individual dishes.

Serves 4
Preparation time:
10 minutes, plus soaking time
Freezing:
Not recommended

TURKISH BEAN SALAD

TURKEY

Served in Turkey as an accompaniment to grilled meats, as a meal on its own with bread, or as part of a *mezze*.

250 g (8 oz) dried haricot beans, soaked overnight
1 clove garlic, crushed
6 tablespoons olive oil
3 tablespoons lemon juice
1 small onion, sliced thinly
1 small green pepper, cored, seeded and sliced thinly

3 tomatoes, peeled and cut into strips
2–3 hard-boiled eggs, each cut into 8 lengthways
8–12 black olives, pitted
2 tablespoons chopped parsley
salt and pepper

Serves 6
Preparation time:
15 minutes, plus soaking time
Cooking time:
1½–1¾ hours
Freezing:
Not recommended

1. Drain the beans and place in a pan of cold water. Bring to the boil and cook rapidly for 10 minutes, then cover and simmer gently for 1¼–1½ hours until tender; add a little salt towards the end of cooking.
2. Drain the beans and place in a bowl. Add the garlic, oil, lemon juice, onion and seasoning, then mix together thoroughly. Set aside to cool.
3. Add the green pepper and tomatoes and toss well.
4. Turn into a serving dish and arrange the eggs and olives around the edge. Sprinkle with parsley to serve.

HORIATIKI

GREECE

This must be the most popular salad in Greece. The name means 'village' salad. It is extremely simple and quick to make and is an ideal accompaniment for Shish Kebab (page 40). It can also be served as a light lunch with warm crusty bread or pitta bread, for mopping up the juices.

½ cucumber, peeled and sliced thinly
1 small onion, sliced thinly into rings
1 green pepper, cored, seeded and cut into rings
500 g (1 lb) tomatoes

4 tablespoons olive oil
1 tablespoon wine vinegar
175 g (6 oz) Feta cheese, cut into cubes
125 g (4 oz) black olives
½ teaspoon dried oregano
salt and pepper to taste

1. Place the cucumber, onion and green pepper in a bowl.
2. Cut each tomato into 8 wedges and add to the bowl with the oil, vinegar, and salt and pepper. Toss thoroughly and turn into a salad bowl.
3. Sprinkle the cheese and olives over the top and dust with a little oregano.

Serves 4
Preparation time: 10 minutes
Freezing: Not recommended

DESSERTS & PASTRIES

ZABAIONE

ITALY

One of the most famous of all Italian sweets, sometimes called *zabaglione*. It is very quick and easy to make, also extremely rich and sweet. It must be made just before serving, as it will separate if left to stand.

4 egg yolks
50 g (2 oz) caster sugar

7 tablespoons Marsala
sponge fingers to serve

Serves 4
Preparation time:
8 minutes
Freezing:
Not recommended

1. Place the eggs and sugar in a bowl and whisk for about 5 minutes, with an electric mixer, over a pan of gently simmering water, until thick and mousse-like.
2. Gradually whisk in the Marsala. Pour into 4 glasses and serve immediately, with sponge fingers.

GRANITA DI MELONE

ITALY

Granitas are said to have originated in Rome, but they are now popular throughout Italy, particularly in Sicily. You can use other mellow summer fruits such as nectarines, peaches or strawberries, instead of melon if you prefer.

125 g (4 oz) sugar
150 ml (¼ pint) water
1 ripe Galia, Ogen or
  Charentais melon

juice of 1 lemon
mint sprigs to decorate

Serves 6
Preparation time:
20 minutes
Freezing time:
About 4 hours

1. Place the sugar and water in a pan and heat gently until dissolved, then boil steadily for 5 minutes. Leave in a cold place to cool.
2. Meanwhile, cut the melon in half, scoop out and discard the seeds. Scoop out the flesh, place in a food processor or blender with the lemon juice and work together until smooth.
3. Stir into the sugar syrup, then turn into a rigid freezer-proof container, cover, seal and freeze for about 3 hours.
4. Whisk and return to the freezer until firm.
5. Leave to stand at room temperature for 10 minutes before serving. Stir until crumbly, spoon into 6 tall glasses and decorate each with a mint sprig.

BRAZO DE GITANO

SPAIN

This delicious filled sponge roll dessert is typical of southern Spain, though its popularity is such that it can now be found in cake shops throughout the country. It is usually served on special occasions.

3 eggs
125 g (4 oz) caster sugar
grated rind of 1 lemon
75 g (3 oz) plain flour,
  sifted
1 tablespoon hot water
caster sugar for dredging

FOR THE FILLING:
2 tablespoons cornflour
175 ml (6 fl oz) milk
1 egg, separated
2 tablespoons sweet sherry
50 g (2 oz) caster sugar

Serves 8
Preparation time:
45 minutes
Cooking time:
10–12 minutes
Freezing:
Not recommended

1. Grease and line a 33 × 23 cm (13 × 9 inch) Swiss roll tin.
2. Whisk the eggs, sugar and lemon rind together with an electric mixer for about 10 minutes, until thick and mousse-like. Carefully fold in the flour, adding the water when almost folded in. Turn into the prepared tin.
3. Bake in a preheated oven, 200°C/400°F/Gas Mark 6, for 10–12 minutes, until the cake springs back when pressed.
4. Wring out a clean tea towel in hot water and lay it on a work surface. Place a sheet of greaseproof paper on top and sprinkle with caster sugar.
5. Turn the sponge out onto the paper and remove the lining paper. Trim off the crisp short sides of the cake, then roll up from one long side with the paper inside the sponge. Place on a wire rack with the join underneath and leave to cool.
6. To make the filling, blend the cornflour with a little of the milk and the egg yolk. Heat the remaining milk to just below boiling point, then pour onto the blended mixture, stirring constantly. Return to the pan, bring to the boil, stirring, and cook for about 2 minutes until thickened, stirring constantly. Remove from the heat and stir in the sherry.
7. Whisk the egg white until stiff, then gradually whisk in the sugar. Fold into the custard.
8. Unroll the sponge and remove the greaseproof paper. Spread the sherry custard filling evenly over the sponge and roll up again. Cut into slices to serve.

FIGUES À L'ORANGE

I think there is no more beautiful fruit than a fresh fig, either purple or green, cut open to reveal the luscious juicy, deep red flesh inside.

FRANCE

6 ripe figs, stalks removed
1 orange

2 tablespoons Grand
Marnier

1. Quarter the figs and place in a large glass dish or divide between 4 glass dishes.
2. Pare the rind thinly from the orange and cut into needle-fine shreds. Blanch for 1 minute in boiling water, then drain.
3. Squeeze the juice from the orange, mix with the liqueur and pour over the figs.
4. Leave to stand for 1 hour to allow the flavours to combine. Sprinkle with the orange shreds to serve.

Serves 4
Preparation time:
10 minutes, plus standing time
Freezing:
Not recommended

ALMOND SPONGE CAKE

GREECE

Known locally as *glykisma amigthalou*, this delicious sponge may be served at coffee time or as a dessert with cream or Greek yogurt.

175 g (6 oz) butter or margarine
125 g (4 oz) caster sugar
3 eggs
300 g (10 oz) self-raising flour, sifted
250 g (8 oz) natural yogurt or 250 ml (8 fl oz) buttermilk

125 g (4 oz) ground almonds
1/2 teaspoon almond essence
FOR THE SYRUP:
350 g (12 oz) caster sugar
250 ml (8 fl oz) water
juice of 1/2 lemon

Cuts into 20 pieces
Preparation time: 15 minutes
Cooking time: About 45 minutes
Freezing: Recommended

Illustrated bottom right

1. Cream the butter or margarine and sugar together until light and fluffy.
2. Beat in the eggs one at a time, adding a tablespoon of flour with the second and third.
3. Fold in the flour alternately with the yogurt or buttermilk, then fold in the almonds and essence.
4. Turn into a greased 30 × 25 cm (12 × 10 inch) baking tin and bake in a preheated oven, 180°C/350°F/Gas Mark 4, for about 45 minutes, until the centre springs back when lightly pressed. Prick the surface with a fork.
5. To make the syrup, heat the sugar and water until dissolved, then boil for 2 minutes. Add the lemon juice. Pour over the cake and leave to cool in the tin.
6. Cut into about 20 pieces to serve.

ALMOND-FILLED PASTRY

MOROCCO

Mehanncha—the Moroccan name for this, literally means 'the snake', and you can see why it is so called. It is very rich, so only serve small portions. In Morocco they use a pastry called *warka*, but fillo gives a similar result.

250 g (8 oz) ground almonds
175 g (6 oz) icing sugar, sifted
1 egg white
1 1/2 tablespoons rose water
1/2 teaspoon almond essence

icing sugar for sprinkling
175 g (6 oz) fillo pastry (6 sheets)
50 g (2 oz) butter, melted
TO FINISH:
icing sugar
cinnamon

1. Mix the ground almonds, icing sugar, egg white, rose water and almond essence together to form a paste. Divide into 3 and roll out each piece on a surface sprinkled with icing sugar into a 48 cm (19 inch) long sausage, just over 1 cm (½ inch) thick.
2. Lay out a sheet of fillo pastry and brush with melted butter. Cover with a second sheet of pastry and brush with more butter.
3. Arrange an almond paste sausage along the length of the fillo pastry, 2.5 cm (1 inch) in from the bottom edge, and roll up.
4. Shape into a loose coil starting in the centre of a greased 20 cm (8 inch) loose-bottomed flan tin.
5. Make 2 more rolls in the same way, join to the first piece in the tin and continue the coil to the edge of the tin.
6. Brush with more butter and bake in a preheated oven, 180°C/350°F/Gas Mark 4, for 30 minutes, until golden.
7. Loosen from the tin, turn upside down and return to the oven for 10 minutes to brown the underside.
8. Invert again onto a serving plate and leave to cool slightly. Dust with icing sugar, then sprinkle cinnamon in lines over the top. Serve warm or cold, cut into wedges.

Cuts into 12 pieces
Preparation time:
30 minutes
Cooking time:
40 minutes
Freezing:
Recommended; heat through in the oven to crisp

Illustrated top left

BAKLAVA

GREECE/TURKEY

This traditionally very sweet dessert is served in many Eastern Mediterranean countries. It has a wonderful flavour, which is in no way impaired by reducing the sweetness a little, as I have done in this recipe. It is very 'more-ish', and the made-at-home kind is much more scrumptious than the ready-made variety.

275 g (9 oz) fillo pastry
(9 sheets)
75 g (3 oz) butter, melted
350 g (12 oz) walnuts or
almonds, chopped finely
50 g (2 oz) breadcrumbs

1 teaspoon ground
cinnamon
½ teaspoon ground cloves
FOR THE SYRUP:
175 ml (6 fl oz) water
250 g (8 oz) sugar
juice of ½ lemon

Cuts into 16 pieces
Preparation time:
30 minutes
Cooking time:
30–35 minutes
Freezing:
Not recommended

1. Grease a 29 × 21 cm (11½ × 8½ inch) baking tin and line with a sheet of pastry.
2. Brush with melted butter, lay another sheet over the top and brush again with butter. Continue until you have 6 layers of pastry. Leave the edges overhanging but trim evenly.
3. Cover the remaining pastry with a damp cloth to prevent it becoming dry and difficult to handle.
4. Mix the nuts, breadcrumbs, cinnamon and cloves together and sprinkle half over the pastry in the baking tin.
5. Cut the remaining 3 fillo sheets in half crossways. Lay 2 pieces of fillo over the nut mixture, brushing each piece with butter. Sprinkle with the remaining nut mixture, then place the remaining 4 pieces of fillo on top, brushing each piece with butter.
6. Fold the bottom overhanging edges neatly over the top, brushing with butter to seal well. Brush the top with the remaining butter. Leave for 5 minutes for the butter to set.
7. Cut lengthways into 4 strips, then cut diagonally to make diamond shapes.
8. Bake in a preheated oven, 180°C/350°F/Gas Mark 4, for 30–35 minutes, until golden.
9. Meanwhile, make the syrup. Place the water and sugar in a pan, bring to the boil, stirring, and continue to boil for 1 minute. Add the lemon juice and leave to cool.
10. Pour the syrup slowly over the baklava in the tin as soon as it is removed from the oven. Leave for about 1 hour until it has all been absorbed. Transfer to a wire rack to cool completely before serving.

AMARETTI

Amaretti, or macaroons, are popular throughout Italy, though they may vary in size from one region to another. They are delicious served with any creamy concoction, and are frequently used crushed to flavour Italian desserts.

ITALY

250 g (8 oz) ground almonds
250 g (8 oz) caster sugar

2 large egg whites (size 1), beaten lightly
2 tablespoons finely chopped almonds

1. Line a baking sheet with baking parchment.
2. Mix the ground almonds and sugar together, then mix in the egg whites.
3. Put the mixture into a piping bag fitted with a large plain nozzle and pipe into 3.5 cm (1½ inch) circles on the prepared baking sheet.
4. Sprinkle with the chopped almonds and bake in a preheated oven, 180°C/350°F/Gas Mark 4, for 15–20 minutes, until golden. Leave to cool on the baking sheet.

Makes about 30
Preparation time:
15 minutes
Cooking time:
15–20 minutes
Freezing:
Recommended

INDEX

Photography by: Andy Seymour
Designed by: Sue Storey
Home economist: Carole Handslip
Stylist: Penny Legg
Illustration by: Linda Smith
Typeset by Rowland Phototypesetting Limited